A Picture Book of
Frederick Douglass

David A. Adler

illustrated by Samuel Byrd

Holiday House / New York

For my nephew Donnie

D.A.A.

For Emily Carroll, the children's librarian at Fitz-
Simons Middle School, Philadelphia, Pennsylvania,
with thanks for her support

S.B.

Text copyright © 1993 by David A. Adler
Illustrations copyright © 1993 by Samuel Byrd
All rights reserved
Printed and bound in March 2019 at Tien Wah Press, Johor Bahru, Malaysia
17 19 20 18
Library of Congress Cataloging-in-Publication Data

Adler, David A.
A picture book of Frederick Douglass / David A. Adler ;
illustrated by Samuel Byrd. — 1st ed.
p.   cm.
Summary: A biography of the man who, after escaping slavery,
became an orator, writer, and leader in the abolitionist movement
in the nineteenth century.
ISBN 0–8234–1002–1
1.   Douglass, Frederick, 1817?–1895—Juvenile literature.
2.   Abolitionists—United States—Biography—Juvenile literature.
3.   Afro-Americans—Biography—Juvenile literature.   4.   Slavery–
–United States—Anti-slavery movements—Juvenile literature.
[1. Douglass, Frederick, 1817?–1895. 2. Abolitionists. 3. Afro–
Americans—Biography.] I. Byrd, Samuel, ill.   II. Title.
E449.D75A35   1993   92–17378   CIP   AC
973.8'092—dc20
[B]
ISBN 0-8234-1205-9 (pbk.)

HOLIDAY HOUSE is registered in the U.S. Patent and Trademark Office.

ISBN-13: 978-0-8234-1002-6 (hardcover)   ISBN-10: 0-8234-1002-1 (hardcover)
ISBN-13: 978-0-8234-1205-1 (paperback)   ISBN-10: 0-8234-1250-9 (paperback)

Frederick Douglass was born a slave on a tobacco, corn, and wheat farm in Talbot County, Maryland. He was born in February 1818. His mother named him Frederick Augustus Washington Bailey.

Frederick's mother was an African-American slave named Harriet Bailey. He never knew who his father was, but he did know that he was a white man. Some people said he was Captain Aaron Anthony, Frederick's first owner.

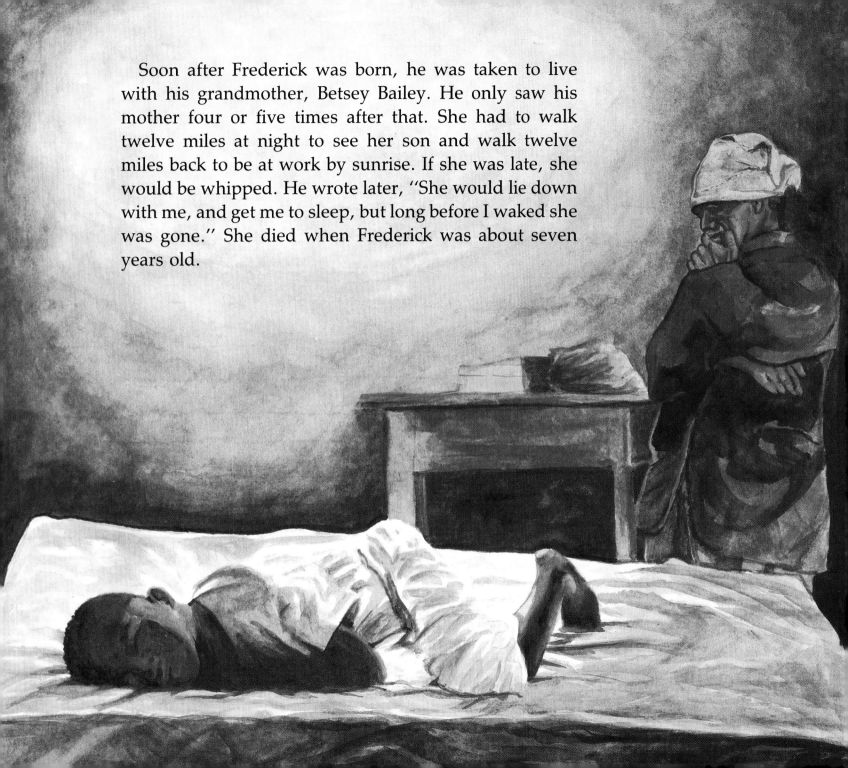

Soon after Frederick was born, he was taken to live with his grandmother, Betsey Bailey. He only saw his mother four or five times after that. She had to walk twelve miles at night to see her son and walk twelve miles back to be at work by sunrise. If she was late, she would be whipped. He wrote later, "She would lie down with me, and get me to sleep, but long before I waked she was gone." She died when Frederick was about seven years old.

When Frederick was six he was taken to his master's house and put to work. He wrote later about how he lived as a slave. "In the hottest summer and coldest winter I was kept almost naked—no shoes, no stockings, no jacket, no trousers, nothing on but a coarse tow linen shirt reaching only to my knees." He was fed boiled corn meal called *mush*.

Frederick was wakened often by the cries of a slave being beaten. The first time that happened it was his own aunt Hester who was tied to a hook and whipped. Young Frederick was so frightened that he ran into a closet and hid.

When Frederick was eight years old he was taken to Baltimore to live as the slave of Sophia and Hugh Auld, relatives of his master's daughter. He ran errands for the Aulds and took care of their infant son, Thomas.

Young Frederick Bailey was Sophia Auld's first slave. She was a good-hearted woman and taught Frederick the alphabet. She began to teach him to read until her husband told her it was against the law. Hugh Auld said a slave "should know nothing but to obey his master."

Sophia Auld stopped teaching Frederick, but he didn't stop learning. He took a book with him when he went out on errands. Poor white boys he met in the street helped him learn to read.

When Frederick was about twelve he told the boys, "I am a slave for life!" and he asked them, "Have not I as good a right to be free as you have?"

Frederick read the Bible and went to a church Sabbath school for black children. When he was fourteen he taught at the school.

In 1833 Frederick was sent to work for Thomas Auld, Hugh's brother. The next year he was sent to work for Edward Covey, a poor farmer known to break the spirit of young slaves. Frederick worked hard. Even so, Covey beat him about once a week. Then, one summer morning, Frederick fought back. Covey never beat him again.

The fight was the turning point in Frederick's life as a slave. "I was nothing before," he said later. "I was a man now."

On January 1, 1835, Frederick was sent to work for William Freeland. On Sundays the slaves had no work, and Frederick opened a secret Sabbath school and taught slaves to read.

Frederick longed to be free. He and a few other slaves hoped to escape by boat. But someone told of their plans, and Frederick was put in jail. He expected to be sold to a slave owner in the Deep South, to work in the cotton fields, a fate Frederick thought of as "a life of living death." But instead he was sent back to Baltimore, to be Hugh Auld's slave again.

Frederick worked in a shipyard. Whatever he earned, he gave to Hugh Auld.

In Baltimore Frederick met with many free African-Americans, including Anna Murray. Together they planned Frederick's escape from slavery.

Frederick planned to travel north by train. Anna gave him the money he needed. A free African-American sailor loaned Frederick papers to prove he was not a slave.

Frederick rode three trains, three ferries, and a steamboat to New York City and freedom. Then, to make it difficult for slave catchers to find him, he changed his surname from Bailey to Johnson, and then to Douglass.

Soon after Frederick arrived in New York, he sent for Anna Murray. They were married on September 15, 1838, and moved further north to New Bedford, Massachusetts. Frederick and Anna Douglass had five children—Rosetta, Lewis, Frederick, Jr., Charles, and Anna.

In New Bedford, Frederick worked loading and un-
loading ships, shoveling coal, and sweeping out chim-
neys. Frederick was pleased he didn't have to share his
wages with a slave owner.

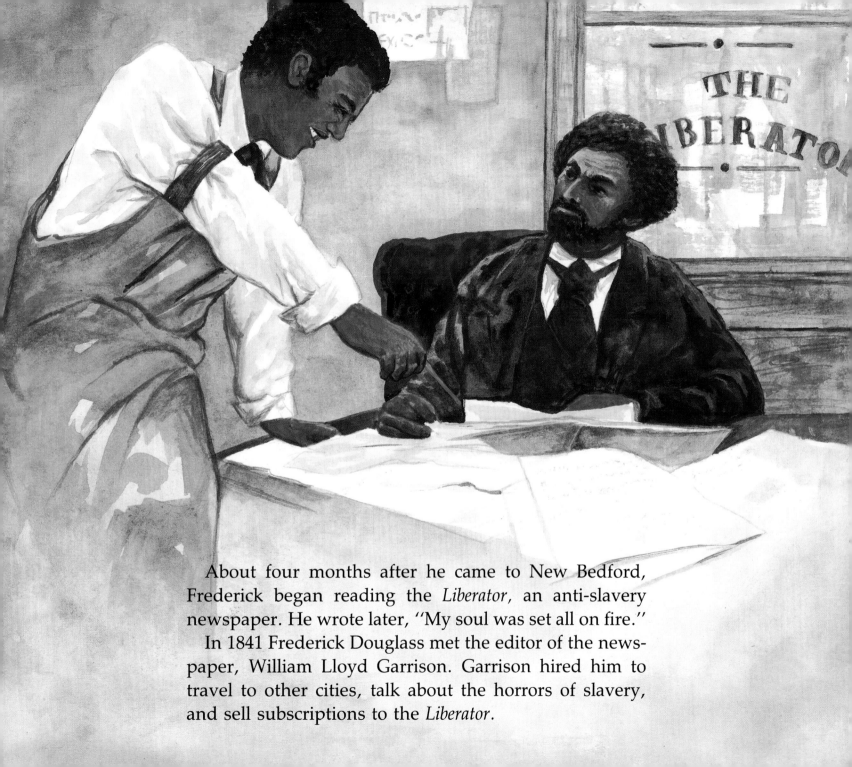

About four months after he came to New Bedford, Frederick began reading the *Liberator*, an anti-slavery newspaper. He wrote later, "My soul was set all on fire."

In 1841 Frederick Douglass met the editor of the newspaper, William Lloyd Garrison. Garrison hired him to travel to other cities, talk about the horrors of slavery, and sell subscriptions to the *Liberator*.

In 1845 his autobiography, *The Narrative of the Life of Frederick Douglass, An American Slave*, was published. In the book he wrote his original name, Frederick Bailey, and the name of his master. This put Frederick in danger of being caught as a runaway slave, so he went to England. He gave speeches there, too, about the evils of slavery.

Frederick Douglass believed that people are not property to be owned by others. But still, in Baltimore, the Aulds held papers proving that they did own him. Some friends in England bought those papers—and his freedom. Now he could go home.

Frederick Douglass returned to the United States in 1847. He moved to Rochester, New York, and started his own anti-slavery newspaper, *The North Star*. Later it was renamed *Frederick Douglass' Paper*.

Frederick spoke out against the racial prejudice he found in the northern states. He spoke out for women's rights. His house became a stop on the Underground Railroad, a series of "safe houses" for runaway slaves on their way further north to freedom.

On April 12, 1861, the four-year-long Civil War between the northern Union army and the southern Confederate army began. It was the war that ended slavery in the United States.

In 1863 Frederick Douglass helped gather soldiers for the first black unit in the Union army. Three of his sons joined. But Frederick Douglass soon learned that black soldiers were paid much less than whites, and were given poor equipment and little training. He told this to President Lincoln. The president told Frederick Douglass to be patient. Progress in the rights of African-Americans would come slowly.

Eight months after the Confederate army was defeated, the Thirteenth Amendment to the United States Constitution was passed. Slavery was outlawed.

In 1864 Abraham Lincoln was reelected president. In March 1865, after the inauguration, Frederick Douglass went to the White House to shake the president's hand. At first he was not allowed in because he was African-American. President Lincoln had him shown in, and as he entered the hall the president said, "Here comes my friend Douglass." Several weeks later, on April 14, President Lincoln was shot. He died the next day.

Frederick Douglass wrote two more books about his life, *My Bondage and My Freedom*, published in 1855, and *The Life and Times of Frederick Douglass*, published in 1881.

In 1877 he was named marshal and in 1881 recorder of deeds for Washington, D.C. In 1889 he was named consul-general to Haiti.

In 1882 Anna Douglass died. Two years later Frederick married Helen Pitts, a white woman.

Both blacks and whites were upset by the marriage. Helen Pitts told people that she had married the man she loved. Frederick Douglass told people that his first wife was black, like his mother. His second wife was white, like his father.

During his last years Frederick Douglass spoke out against the mob violence and lynchings of African-Americans in the south. He wrote that every southern breeze was "tainted and freighted with Negro blood."

Frederick Douglass had helped lead the struggle to end slavery. He had hoped to see blacks and whites throughout the United States living together in peace. He never did. On February 20, 1895, after attending a meeting on women's rights, Frederick had a heart attack and died. He was seventy-seven years old.

IMPORTANT DATES

1818	Born in Talbot County, Maryland. (See author's note.)
1824	Taken to live as a slave of Captain Aaron Anthony.
1826	Sent to live as a slave of Hugh and Sophia Auld in Baltimore, Maryland.
1833	Sent to work as a slave for Thomas Auld.
1834	Fought with his master, Edward Covey.
1835	Sent to work as a slave for William Freeland.
1836	Sent back to his former master Hugh Auld in Baltimore, where he worked in a shipyard.
1838	Escaped to New York. Married Anna Murray.
1841–1845	Worked for William Lloyd Garrison, editor of the *Liberator.*
1845	*Narrative of the Life of Frederick Douglass, an American Slave* was published.
1847	Began his own anti-slavery newspaper, the *North Star*, in Rochester, New York.
1863	Recruited for first black unit in the Union army.
1882	His wife, Anna Murray Douglass, died.
1884	Married Helen Pitts.
1889–1891	Served as American consul-general to Haiti.
1895	Died in Washingon, D.C., on February 20.

AUTHOR'S NOTE

The birthdate of Frederick Douglass and other dates during his slave years are based on current research. A few differ with those given in earlier books, including his autobiography. But even Frederick Douglass was open about his uncertainty concerning them. He once wrote, "I do not remember to have ever met a slave who could tell his own birthday. They seldom come nearer to it than planting-time, harvest-time, cherry-time, spring-time, or fall-time."

Frederick Douglass was known as Frederick Johnson for a very short while, probably no more than two weeks. But it was during that time that he was married. His marriage certificate therefore reads: ". . . joined together in holy matrimony Frederick Johnson and Anna Murray. . . ." Soon after that, in New Bedford, Massachusetts, Frederick changed his name again because he found that the surname Johnson was very common there. In fact, at the time he was staying at the home of a family named Johnson. The name Douglass was taken from a character in the popular novel, *The Lady of the Lake*, by Sir Walter Scott.